Underwater World

SHARKS

By Ryan Nagelhout

 Gareth Stevens
Publishing

Please visit our website, www.garethstevens.com. For a free color catalog of all our high-quality books, call toll free 1-800-542-2595 or fax 1-877-542-2596.

Library of Congress Cataloging-in-Publication Data

Nagelhout, Ryan.
  Sharks / Ryan Nagelhout.
      p. cm. — (Underwater world)
  Includes index.
  ISBN 978-1-4339-8576-8 (pbk.)
  ISBN 978-1-4339-8577-5 (6-pack)
  ISBN 978-1-4339-8575-1 (library binding)
  1. Sharks—Juvenile literature. I. Title.
  QL638.9.N34 2013
  597.3—dc23

                                        2012019203

First Edition

Published in 2013 by
Gareth Stevens Publishing
111 East 14th Street, Suite 349
New York, NY 10003

Copyright © 2013 Gareth Stevens Publishing

Editor: Ryan Nagelhout
Designer: Katelyn Londino

Photo credits: Cover, pp. 1, 17, 23, 24 (clam) iStockphoto/Thinkstock.com; pp. 5, 24 (sea) Hemera/ Thinkstock.com; pp. 7, 13, 24 (teeth) Undersea Discoveries/Shutterstock.com; p. 9 Rich Carey/ Shutterstock.com; p. 11 cbpix/Shutterstock.com; p. 15 © iStockphoto.com/crisod; p. 19 Jim Agronick/ Shutterstock.com; p. 21 Sergey Dubrov/Shutterstock.com.

Printed in the United States of America

CPSIA compliance information: Batch #CW13GS: For further information contact Gareth Stevens, New York, New York at 1-800-542-2595.

Contents

A shark lives in the sea.
This is its home.

It has lots of teeth!
They fall out
all the time!

It has arms
to help it swim.
These are its fins.

There are many kinds.
We know of over 400!

They live many ways.

A whale shark is huge!
It can be
as big as a bus!

It eats little bits of plants.

A great white chases
fish or animals.

A nurse shark lives
at the sea floor.
It likes to eat clams.

A tiger shark eats
anything!

Words to Know

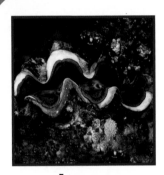
clam

sea

teeth

Index

24